Curtains

DOLLS HOUSE DO-IT-YOURSELF

Curtains

Sue Heaser

David & Charles

To a parfit gentle knight

A DAVID & CHARLES BOOK
David & Charles is a subsidiary of F&W (UK) Ltd.,
an F&W Publications Inc. company

First published in the UK in 2004

Distributed in North America
by F&W Publications, Inc.
4700 East Galbraith Road
Cincinnati, OH 45236
1-800-289-0963

A catalogue record for this book is available from the British Library.

ISBN 0 7153 1852 7 paperback

Printed in Singapore by KHL Printing Co Pte Ltd
for David & Charles
Brunel House   Newton Abbot   Devon

Executive Editor   Cheryl Brown
Editor   Jennifer Proverbs
Art Editor   Prudence Rogers
Designer   Sarah Underhill
Production Controller   Ros Napper
Project Editor   Jan Cutler
Photographer   Karl Adamson
Illustrator   Sue Heaser

Visit our website at www.davidandcharles.co.uk

David & Charles books are available from all good bookshops;
alternatively you can contact our Orderline on (0)1626 334555 or write
to us at FREEPOST EX2110, David & Charles Direct, Newton Abbot
TQ12 4ZZ (No stamp required UK mainland)

DOLLS HOUSE DO-IT-YOURSELF

Curtains

Contents

Introduction

Imagine a home without curtains – what a bleak, unloved place it would seem. The same could surely be said about a dolls' house, but miniature curtains can transform tiny rooms in all kinds of ways. Cheerful cottons printed with rosebuds, and dainty net curtains will add a soft, feminine touch to a bedroom; glossy silks with festoons and fringe will make a miniature Georgian parlour look fit for a king; and a striped roller blind in a bathroom window will make the room look cared for and lived in.

This book will show you how to make beautiful miniature curtains for your dolls' house. The tools and materials used for the projects are all widely available and you will already have many in your home. The Essential Techniques section guides you through the steps of making and draping tiny curtains so that they hang perfectly and you avoid the 'flying in the wind' look that so often spoils dolls' house curtains. The projects give detailed instructions for every popular type of curtain that has been developed through the ages, and there are plenty of tips and advice on how to choose the right style and materials for a dolls' house

of a particular historical period. The projects also include variations, giving you a wide choice of styles to adapt to your own particular dolls' house.

Dolls' houses often have windows only on the opening front wall but it is a shame to make curtains for these windows alone. Many of the projects can be made up as faux curtains: closed curtains or those with a blind as a backing to hide the fact that there is no window. This means that a sumptuous pair of curtains can be fixed to the back wall of a room to provide a richly furnished effect or to enhance a period feel.

Miniature sewing is a delightful hobby and the projects in this book are easily achievable even by a beginner. I have had great delight in researching and designing all the curtains in this book and I hope that you will have even more pleasure in creating them yourself.

How to use this book

Please read the technical sections at the beginning of the book before you start on any projects, and read through the project itself before you begin. Many projects use a standard curtain pattern; you will find full instructions for making the curtains in Essential Techniques on pages 14–22. All the templates and patterns you will need to complete the projects appear on pages 60–63.

Creating Period Style

Curtains are so much part of our homes today that few people realize they are a relatively recent development. Before Tudor times, windows were unglazed and basic and the only way to keep draughts out in colder climates was to cover the window firmly with shutters at night. However, with the development of window glass from the 17th century, people began to drape fabric around the edges of the window frames to decorate and soften them. This gradually developed into curtains as we know them today.

To create an authentic effect it is important to use the correct designs with fabrics and trimmings to suit different historical periods. The following tips will help you to achieve this.

Tudor

Curtains were not used as coverings for windows during Tudor times. However, they were hung in doorways and across rooms to protect against draughts and provide privacy. Bed hangings were common, often made in scarlet fabrics, and tapestries and curtains were hung on the walls for decoration and to provide insulation from cold stone walls.

Colours were rich and warm, with red, green, gold, brown and yellow the most common. Velvet and wool were popular materials for curtains in Tudor times but these are too thick to look convincing for 1:12 scale curtains, so use cotton or silk in rich colours instead. You can sometimes find cotton mini-prints in patterns that suggest Tudor floral embroidery, as shown in the picture.

Georgian (18th century) and Regency (early 19th century)

During the 18th century, fabric draped around windows became fashionable with the central part of the window left uncurtained. By the early 19th century, blinds and sheer curtains began to be part of the show, and valances or swags and tails formed the surround.

Rooms were sparsely furnished during this period, and painted in elegant plain pastel colours. Stripes and plain fabrics were particularly popular for upholstery and curtains. The curtain pole became fashionable towards the end of the 18th century, and during Regency times curtains became ornate with swags and tails, fringes, tassels, tie-backs and cornices.

Projects for Tudor rooms
Hanging Tapestry, page 26; Curtains on a Pole, page 32, hung on walls, across doorways or across a room; Valance Curtains, page 42, used around a four-poster bed, Canopied Bed, page 59.

Projects for Georgian and Regency rooms
Simple Gathered Curtains, page 24; Festoon Blind, page 30, made in sheer fabric; Curtains on a Pole, page 32; Swag and Tails, page 44; Lambrequin, page 48; Elaborate Curtains, page 54.

Victorian

During the 19th century, curtains became even more elaborate with the development of pelmets, valances and lambrequins, often combined with poles, swags, tails, tassels, festoons and cornices. Colours were often dark or strong; patterns were popular, particularly brocades, paisleys, tartans and floral designs.

Projects for Victorian rooms

20th century onwards

After the excesses of the Victorian era, the early 20th century saw a return to simpler styles. Edwardian colours for curtains were usually light and plain with simple pole curtains. Cottage style and art deco followed and both introduced their own distinctive styles. Whereas bold geometric patterns and strong motifs took hold in the 1950s and 1960s, romantic florals and ethnic designs were the hallmark of the 1970s. Modern homes today are often decorated with curtains from all periods. Colours are brighter than ever before and fabric patterns and prints cover an enormous range of styles from pretty florals and folk art to cartoon characters and popular motifs, such as checks, stars, hearts and patchwork.

Projects for 20th century and modern rooms

Glossary

Curtains have a language all to themselves; some of the less well-known words are listed here.

Cornice: a horizontal ornamental moulding fixed above a window (see page 55).

Festoon blind: a blind that is drawn up vertically using several cords that cause the fabric to drape into festoons. Sometimes called an Austrian blind (see page 31).

Finials: the decorative ends of a curtain pole (see page 20).

Lambrequin: a short piece of drapery or pelmet with long sides hung over the top of a window (see page 49).

Net curtains: net or tulle used for an open-weave curtain that is often trimmed with lace (see page 35).

Pelmet: a rigid border of fabric and/or wood above a window, concealing the curtain rail (see page 39).

Sheers: fine, translucent curtains made from organdie or voile or any similar finely woven fabric that is sheer (see page 49).

Swag: a drape of fabric hung horizontally over a window that falls into a curved shape (see page 55).

Tails: folds of pleated fabric that usually hang down on either side of the top of a window (see page 45).

Tie-back: a decorative strip of fabric or cord for holding back a curtain from the window (see page 21).

Valance: a short curtain that is fixed around the top of a window, under a shelf or around a bed frame (see page 43).

Fabrics and Trimmings

To make successful miniature curtains, it is essential to choose fabrics and trimmings that are fine enough to work well in small scale. This section lists the type of fabric and trimmings that are most suitable for miniature curtains.

Plain lawn

Printed lawn

Voile

Printed lawn

Tulle

Fabrics

Fine cotton and silk fabrics are undoubtedly the best for miniature curtains, as they can be made to drape beautifully. Synthetic fabrics are rarely as good, although they can be used successfully for blinds or pelmet coverings where no draping is required.

Most of the following fabrics are readily available from fabric shops and you can usually buy very small lengths. You will need to seek out the tiny prints needed for mini-curtains. Specialist dolls' house haberdashers (see Suppliers, page 64) sell these fabrics in small pieces and patterns that are appropriate for small scale. Quilt-making suppliers are also a good source.

Quantities

All the fabric requirements for the projects in this book are for fabric pieces, which usually measure approximately 23 x 23cm (9 x 9in) when purchased from dolls' house suppliers. However, if you buy fabric by the metre (or yard), you should be able to purchase a 20cm (8in) length, which will be ample for any project.

Tip

To test a fabric to see if it is suitable for miniature curtains, squeeze a fold firmly with your finger and thumb. If the fabric creases easily and holds the crease, it is suitable.

Fabrics to choose

Cotton

- Fine pure-cotton lawn in prints and plains is the easiest fabric for beginners. It does not fray too much and drapes well. Avoid polycotton: it is much harder to drape.
- Quilt and patchwork pieces are an excellent source of tiny patterns.
- Cotton tulle or net is best for net curtains. Avoid tulle made of nylon or polyester because this is difficult to drape.

Silk

- Fine silks, such as pongee, crêpe de Chine and taffeta, are perfect for miniature curtains.
- Slub silk has lines of slub in the weave and makes rather grand miniature curtains for a formal room. Although it is quite stiff, it will drape beautifully.
- Translucent silk, such as georgette, chiffon and the finest pongee are perfect fabrics for sheer curtains.
- Silk jacquard in a fine design resembles brocade, but choose a lightweight one for successful draping.

Fabrics to avoid

- Thick fabrics of any kind, such as wool and velvet, will never drape convincingly in miniature. Even the finest velveteen is the equivalent of 13mm (½in) thick at 1:12 scale, so it is no surprise that velvet dolls' house curtains rarely look convincing.
- While the artificial silks, polyesters and nylons do not fray, they are impossible to drape well in miniature. However, synthetic-fibre fabrics can be used for blinds and to cover pelmets when draping is not required.

Tip

Silk will fray readily so paint fray-preventer on to the cut edges after cutting out the curtains (see page 15).

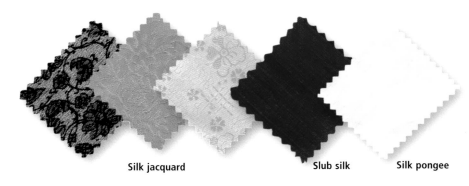

Silk jacquard

Slub silk

Silk pongee

Trimmings

The right trimming can turn plain curtains into a work of art. As with fabrics, it is always important to use trimmings that work well on a miniature scale. Specialist dolls' house haberdashers are a good source of miniature trimmings (see Suppliers, page 64) but you will find many useful mini-trims in ordinary fabric shops as well.

Braid Soutache braid is the narrowest available at 2mm (⅜₂in) wide and this is ideal for trimming around the curved edges of pelmets. To make a ruffled braid, pull one longitudinal thread and the soutache will frill. Picot braid looks like a miniature bobble trim. Fancy braids are useful for trimming formal curtains.

Cord Fine cords are used for tie-backs and trimming.

Fringe This is perfect for curtains with swags and tails and is available from dolls' house haberdashers. Avoid full-size furnishing fringe, which is too large. You can make your own by cutting a narrow strip of fabric, fray-preventing one long edge, and fraying the other.

Lace Pure cotton lace is the easiest to use because it can be folded and draped so well. Lace made from synthetic fibre, such as nylon, seems to have a mind of its own and is difficult to coax into miniature folds and creases. Choose the finest lace you can find or the effect in miniature will be crude. Lace comes in many different widths; use the thinner widths for trimming fabric curtains or for tie-backs. Wider lace can be made into net curtains.

Ribbon Plain pure silk ribbon is available in a wide range of colours and widths and is far easier to use than the widely available polyester ribbon, which is usually too stiff for miniature applications. Use for trimming, bows and tie-backs.

Embroidered ribbon is available in many different designs and is ideal for trimming plain curtains and pelmets.

Tassels Even the tiniest commercial tassels are usually too large for miniatures – see page 22 for how to make your own.

Other trims Tiny silk roses, ribbon bows, charms and beads all make attractive trims for miniature curtains.

Tassels

Cotton lace

Cord

Embroidered ribbon

Purchased miniature fringe

Home-made miniature fringe

Picot braid

Soutache braid

Fancy braids

Double picot braid

Pure silk ribbon

Other Materials and Equipment

You will need a selection of simple tools and other materials to make your miniature curtains, and the main ones are listed here. Specific requirements for a particular project are given in the project.

Materials

The main materials for making miniature curtains are fabrics and trimmings, but you will also need the following materials to complete the projects. All these are easily obtainable from fabric, craft and hobby suppliers.

Card You will need a stiff card (cardstock) for making pelmets and mounting curtains. Card from cereal packets is about the right thickness. Wood or balsa strip, available from hobby suppliers, is an alternative for mounting curtains.

Graph paper is useful for laying on your pinning board (see opposite) before pinning out the curtains; the lines of the paper will help you to keep the curtain edges straight.

Tissue paper is used as a support when sewing very fine fabric on a sewing machine to prevent the tiny pieces from being dragged into the footplate.

Tracing paper is used for making patterns from the templates in the book.

Embroidery floss Six-strand embroidery floss is made of cotton or silk and is used for making tassels (see page 22).

Fray preventer Use PVA (white) glue diluted to the consistency of a thin cream to paint on the raw edges of fabric to prevent fraying. Proprietary liquids, such as Fray Stop, are also available from haberdashers and fabric shops.

Glues Use a white craft glue such as PVA (white) glue or Tacky Glue for all the projects in this book. This type of glue dries clear and flexible, and is ideal for gluing fabrics. It is diluted with water to a thin cream and painted on to the raw edges of fabric with a fine brush to prevent fraying. Use a syringe to squeeze out fine lines of glue for hems and applying trimmings.

Interlining Iron-on bonded interlining is used to stiffen fabric for tie-backs and soft pelmets. Use the lightweight variety for miniature curtains. Iron-on fusible webbing is used for bonding two pieces of fabric together.

Polymer clay This modelling clay comes in a wide range of colours and is baked in an ordinary home oven to a permanent hardness. FIMO and Sculpey are well-known brands. It is perfect for making miniature pole finials and decorations for pelmets.

Spray stiffeners Miniature curtains need to be stiffened after draping in order to keep the folds in place. There are various products available for stiffening fabric, such as spray-on fabric stiffener (for making roller blinds) and spray starch. Firm-hold hairspray also works well. Use these products in a well-ventilated room.

Tape Masking tape is used for assembling pelmets. Double-sided tape is applied to card stiffeners to hold the draped curtains in shape.

Wooden barbecue skewers or dowel is used to make miniature curtain poles. The best thickness is about 3mm (⅛in).

Spray stiffener

Wooden barbecue skewers

Glue

Embroidery floss

Polymer clay

Interlining

Tissue paper

Webbing

Stiff card

Graph paper

Tracing paper

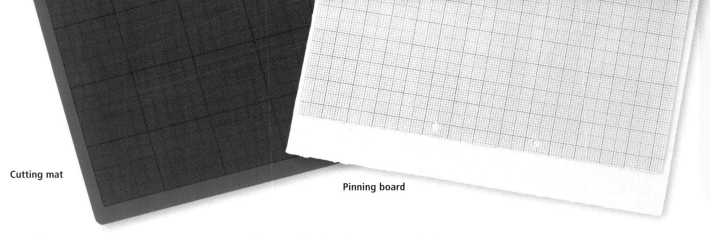

Cutting mat

Pinning board

Equipment

The equipment for making miniature curtains is very basic and you will probably find that you already have most of the things that you need.

Cutting tools A heavy-duty craft knife with a sharp blade, a metal straightedge and a cutting mat or piece of scrap card are all used for cutting out pelmets and card strips. Use the point of a knitting needle to score along the fold lines of pelmets.

Knitting needle Use a long knitting needle or barbecue skewer, about 3mm (⅛in) thick, as the former for pinning folds into miniature curtains on the pinning board.

Pinning board You will need a work board for pinning out miniature curtains into realistic folds, festoons and swags. You can use the back of an expanded polystyrene ceiling insulation tile. These are inexpensive and are available in packs from hardware and home improvement stores. Cardboard from large grocery cartons, a cork tile, or a piece of foam core board are also suitable – in fact anything flat that can take pins. The

polystyrene of ceiling tiles can react with the spray stiffeners, so cover the tile with clear film (plastic wrap) or graph paper before use.

Pins Use ordinary stainless steel or brass dressmaker's pins to pin out your curtains.

Sewing equipment

Sharp scissors are essential. Invest in a pair of good quality sharp scissors and use them only for cutting fabric. You will need some small embroidery scissors as well.

Needles are used for hand-sewing hems and gathers.

Polyester thread is finer than pure cotton thread and is less likely to break when you are pulling up gathering threads.

Sewing machine Although useful, a sewing machine is not essential because you can sew by hand instead (see pages 16–17).

Syringe A syringe with a fine nozzle is ideal for applying tiny quantities of glue exactly where you want it. They are available from craft suppliers and pharmacies.

Basic Tool Kit

These tools are needed for virtually every project and are listed in the You Will Need section as 'Basic Tool Kit':

Cutting tools for card
Dressmaker's pins
Paintbrush
Pinning board
PVA (white) glue
Ruler
Sewing equipment
Sharp pencil
Spray stiffener
Tape – double sided and masking tape
Thin card (cardstock) for backing strips for the curtains

Craft knife

Sharp scissors

Polyester thread

Knitting needle

Pins

Needles

Syringe

Essential Techniques

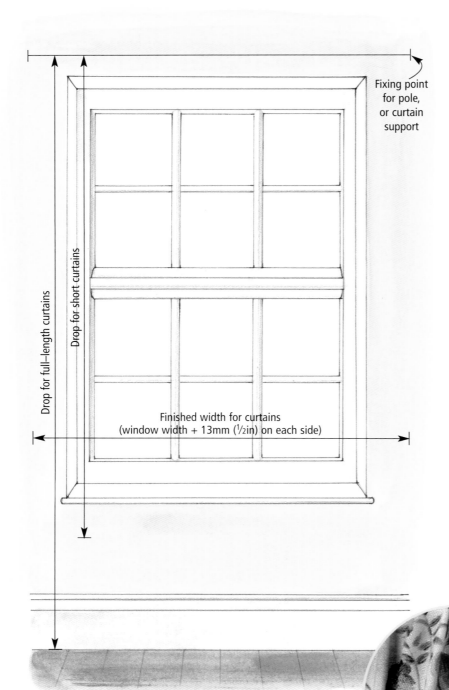

Fixing point for pole, or curtain support

Drop for full-length curtains

Drop for short curtains

Finished width for curtains
(window width + 13mm (1/2in) on each side)

Remember to allow for any trim on the curtain or valance edges when measuring up.

Measuring miniature windows

All the patterns given in this book are based on the scale of 1:12, which is the most popular scale for dolls' houses. If your dolls' house is in another scale, such as 1:16 or 1:24, you will need to adjust the patterns accordingly.

Window sizes

Most dolls' houses have similar window sizes, although these will depend on the period of the dolls' house. The patterns in this book are based on the standard-sized dolls' house window of approximately 9.5 x 13.5cm (3¾in x 5½in). Many of the more elaborate curtains are floor length. If your windows are very different in size, you will need to adjust the length and width.

A good rule of thumb for miniature curtains is to cut the fabric approximately twice the width of the window. This gives generous gathers and allows the side edges to be turned under by 3mm (⅛in) for a neat finish. The curtains should be gathered so that they extend beyond the sides of the window by about 13mm (½in) on each side and be fixed about 10mm (⅜in) above the top of the window frame. The length of fabric to allow is the required drop plus allowance for hems at top and bottom, if required. Allow a bottom hem of 13mm (½in). If the bottom edge is to have a trimming, no hem is needed. The allowance at the top of the curtain will vary according to the project.

Cutting out patterns

It is difficult to cut out tiny pieces of fabric in the conventional way where the pattern is pinned to the fabric and then cut around. The following technique will help you to cut out the pieces accurately.

Iron the fabric well. Lay the pattern on the fabric and draw around it with a sharp pencil. (Dark fabrics are best marked with a chalk pencil.) You can then cut out the curtain accurately along the marked lines.

Fabrics that fray easily, such as silk, should be painted with diluted PVA (white) glue along the lines before cutting out (see Fray Control).

Tip

When cutting out fabrics with a bold pattern, take care that the lines of pattern match across both curtains.

Fray control

Before you start to make up the curtains it is important to prevent the raw edges fraying on such small pieces of fabric.

Use PVA (white) glue diluted to a thin-cream consistency or use a proprietary brand of liquid fray-preventer to paint along the raw edges using a fine paintbrush.

A thin coat of diluted glue painted over the surface of the fabric allows you to cut out elaborate scallops and tabs such as in the Café Curtain project (see page 50).

Making the curtains

Miniature curtains are best made with a combination of gluing and sewing so that the visual effect is as much to scale as possible.

Hemming

You can hem miniature curtains with glue or stitching. A fine line of glue is usually best because this is the least visible. Hem miniature curtains first at the sides, then along the bottom edge using a single turn to avoid bulk.

1 First press down the hem, and then apply a thin line of glue under the turning using a syringe, and press down lightly. Alternatively, sew with a line of fine machine stitches or by hand with a hemming stitch that only just catches the front of the fabric.

2 Lightly glue hems on tulle net curtains so that a line of stitching does not show through the fabric. For fine silk and organdie curtains, test the glue on a scrap of waste fabric first; the glue may show through some extremely sheer fabrics, so hand-hemming is best for these.

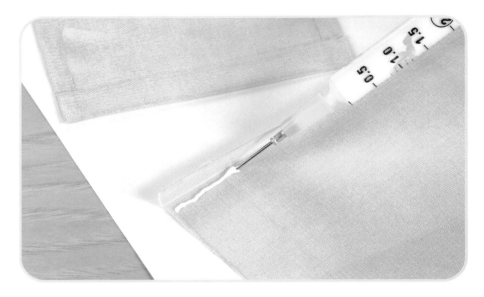

Applying trim

Add miniature trims before you make up the curtains. Use PVA (white) or craft glue, rather than sewing, to avoid stiffness, and apply with a glue applicator or syringe with a fine tip. Lightly mark the line to be glued with a ruler and pencil first, if you find it difficult to keep the line straight.

A decorative trim will finish curtains and blinds attractively. Using glue ensures a neat finish, as shown on this Roller Blind from page 28.

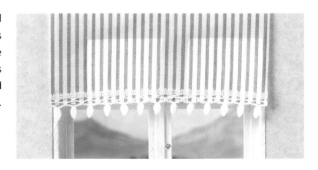

Using glue on the side turnings avoids unsightly stitches showing through nets. (See page 34 for how to make these Classic Net Curtains.)

Gathering and draping

Realistic miniature curtains need to fall naturally in gentle folds, exactly like the real thing. To do this, the fabric must be firmly controlled to prevent the 'flying in the wind' look that some dolls' house curtains have. The following steps show you how to make beautifully draped miniature curtains that hang like real ones.

Gathering

Once the curtain is hemmed, the top edge needs to be gathered. Curtains that will have their headings on view need to have the top edge turned down by 10mm (⅜in). Curtains with headings hidden behind pelmets, valances and swags, can be gathered between 3mm (⅛in) and 6mm (¼in) from the raw top edge.

Machine sewing

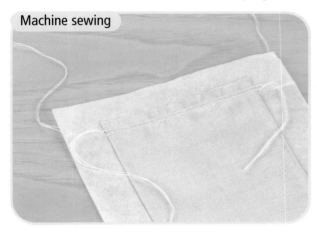

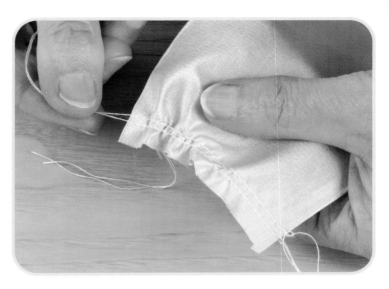

1 Set your machine to a long stitch and sew a line of gathering stitches 6mm (¼in) from the top edge, and another line 1.5mm (¹⁄₁₆in) from the first. If the fabric is very fine, lay it on tissue paper and sew through the fabric and the paper. The paper is easy to tear away afterwards.

2 Gather the curtain by pulling the top threads at one side and pushing the fabric towards the centre. Repeat for the other side, arranging the gathers evenly, until the curtain is the desired width. Tie off the threads to secure.

Hand sewing

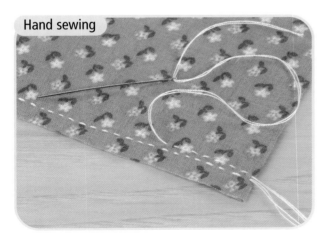

This Festoon Blind (see page 30) has vertical gathers as well as gathers along the top edge to give it fullness.

Use doubled thread and run a line of small running stitches along the two lines to be gathered as for machine stitching above. Gather by pulling on the threads at each side as before.

Gathering is used in the valance as well as the curtains for this bay window (see page 52).

Draping

This method of draping miniature curtains is simple and quick to do. It gives a natural result and requires no special equipment such as a pleater. The instructions below show how to drape a single curtain using a pinning board. For a matching pair, pin and drape the second curtain to the board beside the first.

1 Lay the curtain on to a pinning board that has been covered with graph paper. Pin in place along the top edge. Pin down the left side of the curtain, keeping along a line on the graph paper. Place a knitting needle under the fabric, pushing it against the pinned edge and tuck the fabric into a fold around it, pinning it down along its length at several points. Repeat to make another fold.

2 After the first two folds are pinned down, pin down the right side of the curtain, again keeping it straight along a line of the graph paper and ensuring that the bottom edge is horizontal. Now continue making folds across the curtain, working from left to right towards the pinned right-hand side and adjusting the final few folds so that they fit.

3 Hold a steam iron over the fabric and steam (or use a kettle). Leave to dry and then spray generously with spray starch or hairspray to stiffen. When completely dry, remove from the board.

4 To hold the folds in the curtain, apply a strip of double-sided tape to a piece of card 20mm (¾in) wide that is cut the same width as the curtain. Press the lower folds against the tape so that they are held firmly and cannot spread out.

Draping for tie-backs

If your curtains are to have tie-backs, you will need to drape the curtains into the correct shape so that they appear to hang naturally from the tie-back.

1 Follow steps 1–2 of the instructions for draping a normal curtain. Steam but do not stiffen. Remove the pins from the lower part of the half of the curtain that is to be on the inside edge of the window. From a point about one-third of the way up the inner edge, push the folds up and outwards, gathering the curtain into a festoon.

2 Pin the curtain into its new shape, belling the fabric out above where the tie-back will be positioned and keeping the outside edge pinned straight. The inside bottom of the curtain will rise up a little and should be pinned in place too.

3 Repeat to drape the second curtain alongside the first so that it mirrors the first, using the graph-paper lines as a guide. Steam both curtains and stiffen with spray starch or hairspray. Tie-backs can now be sewn or glued in place around the curtains (see page 21). Card strips to hold the folds are not usually needed for the backs of curtains with tie-backs.

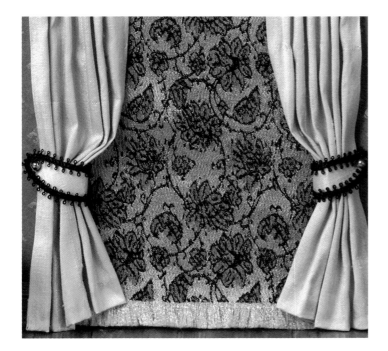

Careful draping of curtains for tie-backs gives them a wonderfully luxurious appearance that is just like full-sized curtains. See page 54 for these sumptuous Elaborate Curtains.

Attaching curtains to the dolls' house window

The simplest way to attach miniature curtains to the dolls' house window is to glue the curtains to a thin strip of wood or card and glue this to the wall above the window. The projects give instructions for attaching different types of curtains to dolls' house windows. Faux curtains can simply be glued to the wall of the room.

Curtain poles

Miniature curtain poles are available from dolls' house suppliers, but it is not difficult to make your own and then you can have great fun varying the colours and finials to suit the period or colour scheme of your dolls' house room.

Simple curtain pole – with ball finials and rings

This is a basic pole that you can cut to length to fit your dolls' house window. You can paint the pole any colour you like and use matching polymer clay for the finials and coloured wire for the rings. See page 32 for how to make Curtains on a Pole. You will need approximately 12 rings for a 12.5cm (5in) long pole. Rings should be spaced about 10mm (⅜in) apart.

You will need

Polymer clay in beige or light brown

Smooth ceramic tile

About 15cm (6in) of 18 gauge (0.7mm) gold-plated jewellery wire

Paintbrush handle or dowel, slightly thicker than the pole (about 5mm (³⁄₁₆in) thick)

Cutting pliers

Wooden dowel or a wooden barbecue skewer about 3mm (⅛in) thick, cut to the measurement of the width of the window plus 25mm (1in)

Superglue

1 To make the finials, knead a walnut-sized piece of polymer clay until it is soft, and roll it into a 5mm (³⁄₁₆in) thick log. Cut several 1mm (¹⁄₃₂in) thick slices. Form each slice into a little ball and press down on to the tile to make disks about 3mm (⅛in) across.

2 Cut several 5mm (³⁄₁₆in) lengths and roll into balls. Press one on each disk. Add a tiny ball to the top of each finial. Bake on the tile for 15 minutes at 130°C/275°F/Gas ½ or according to the instructions on the packet.

Cast-iron pole

This type of pole looks perfect in a Tudor dolls' house.

Use black polymer clay for the fleur-de-lis finials and black wire for the rings. Paint the curtain pole black. Form 6mm (¼in) balls of black clay into teardrops and press down on to the tile. Make a cut on either side of the point as shown and bend each side out and down into a curve. Trim the base of each finial and press on a small oval to finish. Bake as above and glue to the end of the pole after threading on the rings.

3 To make the rings, wind the wire around the paintbrush handle or dowel. Slide the coiled wire off the paintbrush and cut along the centre top of the coil with the cutting pliers, one ring at a time. The rings will be slightly open so bend the ends together. Thread them on to the pole. Glue the finials on to the ends of the pole. See individual projects for hanging instructions.

Tie-backs

Miniature curtains look wonderful with tie-backs, which are the perfect finishing touch. They can be made in many different ways, from a simple cord tied around the curtain to a richly trimmed fabric shape. Before attaching tie-backs, you will need to drape and spray the curtains for tie-backs (see page 19).

Bow tie-backs

This is the simplest way to make a tie-back: just tie a length of ribbon or cord around the draped and stiffened curtain at the narrowest point, with the bow arranged attractively at the front. A dab of glue on the ends of the ribbon will prevent fraying.

Lace and ribbon tie-backs

Wrap the lace or ribbon around the draped and stiffened curtain at the narrowest point of the drape. Cut to length and trim the ends at an angle as shown. Stitch the ends together and sew a gold-coloured bead to the top outer edge to suggest a fixing point. Paint the raw edges with dilute glue to prevent fraying.

Variations

Print tie-backs: make these in a matching fabric to the main curtains or as a contrast to plain curtains. Make the tie-backs as below and glue ribbon to the top edge of each and fringe to the bottom edge. Attach a matching bead for each fixing point.

Tasselled tie-backs: make plain silk tie-backs and glue contrasting cord around the edges. Attach tassels (see page 22) to the ends instead of beads.

Red and gold tie-backs: make plain red silk tie-backs. Glue fancy gold braid around the edges and attach gold-coloured beads.

Fabric tie-backs

This type of tie-back looks particularly pleasing and can be made either in a matching or contrasting fabric.

You will need

Tie-back template (page 62)

Iron-on interlining

Fabric

Trimming (use a braid or cord trim that can be curved around the tie-back without folding)

Beads, for fixings

PVA (white) glue

1 Make a card template from the pattern. Draw around the card template twice on to the interlining to mark the tie-back shape. Iron the interlining on to the back of the fabric, and cut out the tie-backs.

2 Glue the trimming all around the edges of the tie-backs. Wrap each tie-back around the curtain and stitch the ends together, sewing on a bead to finish. When the curtains are glued in place on the window, glue the outer end of the tie-back to the wall.

Making miniature tassels

Miniature tassels make sumptuous trimmings for dolls' house curtains. It is virtually impossible to buy commercially made tassels that are small enough for dolls' house-scale furnishings but it is easy to make them yourself. These instructions are for tassels that are 10mm (⅜in) long: the equivalent of 11.5cm (4½in) long at 1:12 scale.

You will need

Stiff card (cardstock),
25mm (1in) wide strip, about 7.5cm (3in)
long and folded in half

6-strand embroidery floss
in cotton or silk

Sharp scissors

Needle

1 Starting from the bottom of the card strip, and using all six strands of floss, wind the floss around the card eight times. Slip the scissors into the gap between the doubled card and snip through the floss.

2 Lay the little hank on your work surface with the threads aligned. Thread a needle with two strands of floss about 15cm (6in) long. Tie the end of this tightly around the centre of the hank in a double knot.

3 Pull the strands of floss all around the tying thread to make the tassel skirt. Use the tying thread to bind the tassel tightly 1.5mm (1/16in) from the end. Push the needle through the binding twice to secure it and then bring the needle up through the top of the tassel again to provide a hanging thread.

4 Trim the tassel skirt with sharp scissors so that all the strands are the same length. The tassel can now be sewn to curtains using the tying thread.

Attaching tassels to a cord

To attach a tassel to a cord for tie-backs or hanging tassels, tie a knot in the end of the cord and lay it on the floss hank with the knot just over halfway down. Tie the hank tightly around the centre as above, trapping the knotted cord. Pull the skirt down all around the cord and bind and finish the tassel as before.

Basic Curtain Styles

Simple Gathered Curtains

These pretty curtains are quick and easy to make and are an ideal beginner's project. They are gathered by simply threading them on to the pole and pushing the fabric into gathers. Fine cotton lawn is the easiest fabric to use – choose a delicate print to match your dolls' house room decor. They look equally pretty made up as full-length curtains.

You will need

Basic Tool Kit (see page 13)

Fine cotton fabric in a small print

Wooden skewer or dowelling, 3mm (⅛in) diameter

2 small screw eyes or hooks large enough to take the skewer or dowelling

2 finials (see page 20)

Variation

Simple gathered curtains can be made full length as well. They can also be adapted for a gathered café curtain by making them half-length and gluing the pole across the centre of the window.

Tip

When sewing the casing for the skewer, be careful not to make it too tight or you will be unable to insert the skewer. A snug fit is best so that the gathers are neat but the fabric can be pushed along the skewer without difficulty.

1 Measure the window and cut two pieces of fabric, each as wide as the width of the window and the length of the drop required plus 25mm (1in). Fray-check the edges (see page 15) and sew or glue a hem of 3mm (⅛in) along the sides of each curtain and a 13mm (½in) hem along the bottom edges.

2 Press down a 13mm (½in) hem at the top of each curtain. Sew a line of fine stitching 1.5mm (¹⁄₁₆in) from the raw edge of the hem. Place the skewer or dowelling in the resulting casing and push it against the stitching with the side of a ruler. Mark a line between the ruler and the skewer with the pencil. Remove the skewer and sew along the line to make a snug casing that fits the skewer.

3 Thread both curtains on to the skewer and push the sides of each together to gather them up to about one-third of their original width. Cut the skewer to the width of the window plus 25mm (1in). Push the gathered curtains to about 6mm (¼in) from the skewer ends.

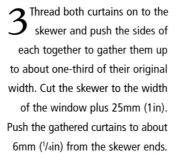

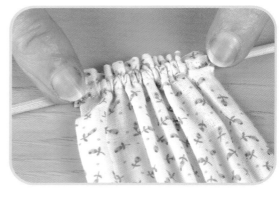

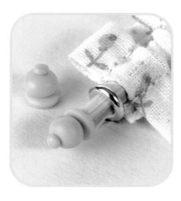

4 With the curtains still on the skewer, pin the gathered top edges to the pinning board. Follow the instructions on page 18 to drape and starch the curtains into folds, and tape card strips to their backs. Screw the screw eyes into the wall above the window so that they hold the skewer 6mm (¼in) from each end. Insert the ends of the skewer and glue on the finials. The card at the back of the curtains can be glued to the wall if necessary to hold the curtains in place.

Hanging Tapestry

In Tudor times curtains for windows had not been invented, but all the best Tudor houses had hanging tapestries displayed on their walls both for decoration and adding warmth to the room. This miniature tapestry has a sumptuous fringe and a 'wrought iron' pole with fleur-de-lis finials, which can easily be adapted for dolls' houses of all periods.

You will need

Basic Tool Kit (see page 13)

Tapestry illustration and tabs (page 61)

Pale blue fabric to match the tapestry

Wooden skewer or dowelling, 3mm (⅛in) diameter, painted black and trimmed to 10cm (4in) long

Two black fleur-de-lis finials (see page 20)

Tip

Weavings and embroideries, either ancient or modern, will look effective made in this way. You can find reproductions of samplers, tapestries or embroideries on the Internet or in books that contain historical fabrics from your library. You could even copy a reproduction of a modern wall hanging to use in a 21st-century dolls' house.

1 Use a colour photocopier to copy the tapestry illustration and tabs on to plain paper. (Alternatively, you can scan the picture on to your computer and print it with a colour printer.) Cut out the tapestry and tabs.

2 Spread the back of the tapestry print with PVA glue and press it firmly on to the fabric, ensuring that it is straight with the fabric grain. When the glue is dry, cut around the image, leaving a 13mm (½in) border of fabric at the bottom.

3 Use the point of a dressmaker's pin to pick loose a few of the horizontal threads from one end of the bottom border. Pull them out and repeat to fray the bottom edge into a 10mm (⅜in) fringe.

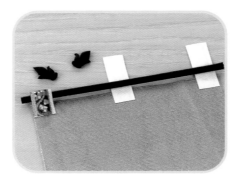

4 Turn the tapestry over and glue the bottom front of each of the three tabs to the top back of the fabric. Lay the wooden skewer or dowelling across the tabs and glue them down over it. Glue the finials to the ends of the skewer and glue it to the wall so that the tapestry hangs straight.

Roller Blind

Simple to make in miniature, roller blinds add a delightful finishing touch to dolls' house kitchens and bathrooms that date from Victorian times to the present day. They were also used in Victorian formal rooms, full length to the floor, and made of toning or cream fabric hung behind draped curtains with tie-backs and a pelmet, valance or cornice (see pages 54–57).

You will need

Basic Tool Kit (see page 13)

Fine cotton or silk fabric (see Tip)

Interlining (optional)

Wooden skewer or dowelling, 3mm (1/8in) diameter

Lace or trimming

Waxed thread (see Tip)

Bead, 1.5mm (1/16in) diameter, in a colour to match fabric

Tips

• When the fabric has a reverse side, bond it back to back with fusible webbing so that the rolled up section matches the front
• If you don't have any waxed thread to attach to the blind, you can pull a length of sewing thread against the side of a candle to coat it in wax.

1 Adjust the pattern to fit the width of the window. Iron the fabric and draw around the pattern, taking care that any fabric pattern is kept symmetrical and straight. Paint along the pencil lines with dilute PVA glue (see page 15); allow to dry, and cut out. If the fabric is very fine, iron a strip of interlining on to the bottom of the back of the fabric to hold it rigid.

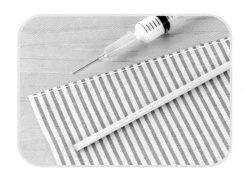

2 Cut a length of skewer or dowelling the same width as the fabric. Apply a line of glue to the top edge of the front of the fabric. Roll the skewer up in the fabric for several turns, as far as the marked line on the pattern, keeping the edges flush and the skewer parallel to the bottom of the fabric.

3 Apply another thin line of glue just below the rolled up skewer and roll it on to this to hold it in place. Weight it with a ruler to prevent it unrolling, and leave to dry.

4 Glue a length of lace or trimming to the bottom edge of the blind. Knot the end of the waxed thread and thread on the bead. Stitch the thread to the centre bottom of the blind, allowing it to hang down about 20mm (3/4in). Glue the rolled blind to the top of the window.

Festoon Blind

Also known as Austrian blinds, festoon blinds have been popular since Georgian times and are not difficult to make in miniature with the help of the pinning board. The project shows how to make a blind that is partly raised to give the full effect of the festoons. This type of blind could be used with a pelmet and draped curtains for an elaborate Victorian-style window.

You will need

Basic Tool Kit (see page 13)

Fine cotton fabric

Cardboard or wood strip, 6mm (¼in) wide and as long as the width of the window

2mm (³⁄₃₂in) wide soutache braid in a contrasting colour

1 Measure the window and cut out the fabric in a rectangle, 5cm (2in) longer than the height of the window and twice the width. Fray-check all the edges (see page 15). Sew a single vertical line of gathering stitches in the centre of the blind and two more, each 3mm (⅛in) from each side. Sew a line of gathering stitches 3mm (⅛in) from the top edge, and another 1.5mm (¹⁄₁₆in) below this.

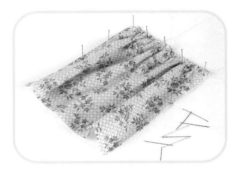

2 Pull the pairs of horizontal threads to gather the top of the blind to the width of the window (see page 17), arranging the gathers evenly. Pin this top edge to the pinning board and then pin and drape the upper half of the blind into folds (see page 18).

3 Pull up the vertical gathering threads at the bottom of the blind to gather the bottom half of the blind, leaving the pinned upper half ungathered. Coax the fabric into festoons with a scalloped bottom edge and pin to the board down each line of gathers, keeping the sides vertical. Steam and spray as usual.

4 Remove from the board when dry and glue the top edge of the blind to the strip of wood or card. Glue a line of braid to the scalloped bottom edge of the blind and a bow of braid to the bottom centre. Attach a card strip to the lower part of the blind to hold the gathers in place. Glue the blind to the window.

Curtains on a Pole

Curtains suspended from a pole look particularly pleasing in miniature and can be adapted for most period styles. You can make the miniature curtain poles and finials yourself or use purchased poles. The curtains can be long or short, or used as a faux window display mounted on the back wall of a dolls' house room.

You will need

Basic Tool Kit (see page 13)

Standard long curtain pattern (see page 60)

Fine cotton fabric

Brass curtain pole with rings (purchased, or see page 20)

2 small screw hooks

Variation

Curtains on a pole are perfect for Tudor dolls' houses, and medieval paintings occasionally show this type of curtain being used to screen off the part of a room containing a bed. For a Tudor effect, use scarlet fabric and trim the bottom with gold fringe. To finish, hang tassels from the sides.

1 Cut out two curtains using the standard long curtain pattern and hem the sides and bottom of each. Press down the top edge and sew a line of gathering stitches 1.5mm (1/16in) from the folded top edge and another 1.5mm (1/16in) below that. Pull up the gathers so that the two curtains fit the width of the window with about 13mm (1/2in) extra on either side. Fasten off.

4 Stitch the gathered top of the curtains to the rings on the pole, spacing them evenly and positioning them so that the top edge of the curtain hangs just below the pole with the rings visible. Screw the hooks to the wall of the dolls' house and hang the curtain pole on them. The card backing at the bottom of the curtains can be glued to the wall as well.

2 Pin the gathered top edge of the curtain to a pinning board and use a knitting needle to create folds, pinning between each and keeping the sides vertical and the top and bottom horizontal (see page 18). Steam and stiffen, then repeat for the second curtain.

3 When the curtains are dry, remove the pins. Cut two pieces of card, each the width of the gathered curtain by 20mm (3/4in), and apply a strip of double-sided tape to each. Press each on to the back of each curtain, about 25mm (1in) from the bottom hem, to hold the folds in place.

Classic Net Curtains

Net curtains are always popular in dolls' houses. Their frothy whiteness makes the windows look homely and pretty when viewed from both the outside and the inside. This project shows a quick and easy way to make lace curtains that hang beautifully. Choose a fine lace to trim the curtains and work on a dark background so that the sheer fabric is easier to see. See page 36 for further ideas for different styles of net and sheer curtains.

You will need

Basic Tool Kit (see page 13)

Fine white cotton tulle or net

Fine white lace, 25mm (1in) wide by about 40cm (16in) long

White silk ribbon, 1.5mm (^{1}/16in) wide by 20cm (8in) long

Strip of stiff card (cardstock), 6mm (^{1}/4in) wide and 13mm (^{1}/2in) longer than the width of the window

Tip

Prepare your pinning board for working with net by pinning a dark piece of fabric over it instead of the graph paper.

1 Measure the window and cut out two pieces of fabric, each the width of the window and the length of the drop required less 25mm (1in). Glue a length of lace to the bottom of each curtain. Fold under a 5mm (^{3}/16in) hem down each side of the curtains, iron firmly and glue lightly.

3 Sew two lines of gathering stitches through all thicknesses of lace and curtain 6mm (^{1}/4in) from the top edge. Pull the top threads to gather the curtains until they are 13mm (^{1}/2in) wider than the width of the window.

2 Lay the remaining lace face down on a work surface. With the right side facing the work surface, lay the top edge of one curtain on top of the lace, aligning the edge of the curtain with the end of the lace and the top raw edge of the curtain just below the top edge of the lace. Lay the second curtain over the first, overlapping by about 13mm (^{1}/2in) and trim the lace to length. Apply glue to the ends of the lace to prevent fraying.

4 Pin the gathered top of each curtain to the pinning board and arrange the folds, forming the curtains into a tie-back shape. Tie a ribbon bow around each curtain for a simple tie-back. Steam, stiffen and leave to dry. Remove from the board and glue the top edge of the curtains to the card strip. Glue this to the wall above the window.

Sheer Inspiration

Many of the basic curtain projects in this book can be adapted to make a variety of delightful net and sheer curtains for dolls' house windows. Some suggestions are given below.

Simple gathered nets

Make net curtains, trimmed with lace, as for the Simple Gathered Curtains on page 24. Make a white pole and finials and thread the curtains on to the pole, gathering them to fit the window. Drape for tie-backs and use lace to make the tie-backs.

Café net curtain

Use fine cotton net or tulle and cut out a curtain twice the width of the window and half the drop plus 25mm (1in). Make up and drape as for the Simple Gathered Curtains on page 24, gathering the curtain to the width of the window on a gold-painted pole. Attach the pole to the window approximately halfway up.

Single sheer curtain with pelmet and drapes

This type of curtain gives a rich result that would suit a Regency or Victorian dolls' house and is used as a backing for a faux window. Cut out a single curtain in sheer organdie or silk using the standard long curtain pattern (page 60) but doubling the width. Make and drape the curtain in the usual way (see pages 16–18), gathering it to approximately 11.5cm (4½in) wide. Glue the gathered top to a card support. Make curtains with a pelmet following the instructions on page 38 and glue these over the sheer curtain.

Double sheer curtains on a pole

This type of curtain is ideal for a modern dolls' house. Use a sheer fabric such as cotton voile or silk pongee. Make the curtains as for Curtains on a Pole on page 32 and glue a line of lace down the inside edge of each. Drape for tie-backs and sew on lace tie-backs.

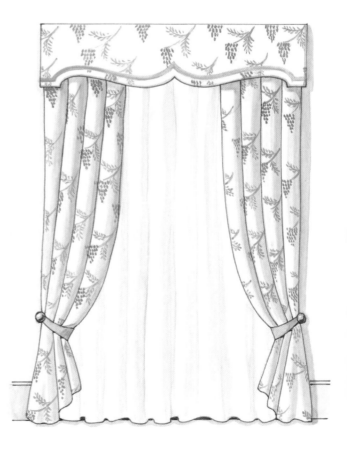

Creative Curtain
Styles

Curtains with a Pelmet

The Victorians adored elaborate window dressings with tassels, tie-backs and pelmets. Although grand pelments went out of fashion during the 20th century, they are popular again today so this style would also be suitable for formal rooms in a modern dolls' house. This sophisticated design is easy to make and you can add more tassels and trims if you wish for a more opulent look.

You will need

Basic Tool Kit (see page 13)

Standard long curtain pattern (page 60) and pelmet template (see page 62)

Slub silk fabric

30cm (12in) gold picot trim

2 gold-coloured beads

2 gold tassels (see page 22)

Stiff card (cardstock)

1 Cut out the curtains using the standard long curtain pattern and make according to the instructions on pages 14–17. Pull up the gathers to make each curtain about 13mm (½in) wider than half the width of the window. Fasten off. Pin the curtains to a pinning board and shape into folds with a knitting needle, draping each into a festoon for tie-backs. Steam and stiffen.

2 Make tie-backs with the picot trim, and glue in place, holding the ends in position with a dressmaker's pin until dry. Glue a gold bead to each tie-back to suggest a decorative hook and stitch a tassel to the centre front. When dry, remove the curtains from the board. Cut a strip of card 25mm (1in) wider than the window by 10mm (⅜in) and glue the gathered tops of the curtains to this.

3 Trace and cut out the pelmet from stiff card, using the craft knife to cut around the curves. Score along the lines indicated. Fold to shape and tape together with masking tape.

4 Cut a piece of fabric about 6mm (¼in) larger all round than the pelmet. Spread a thin layer of PVA glue over the pelmet and press on the fabric, snipping into the curves and corners and gluing the excess fabric tightly to the back.

5 Glue the picot trim along the edges of the pelmet. Glue the card strip with the curtains attached to the wall above the window and glue the pelmet over this. For a faux window, make a full-length blind (see page 28) and glue this to the wall with the curtains and pelmet over the top.

Scalloped Art Deco Pelmet

This project shows you how to adapt a geometric patterned fabric to make a matching pelmet and curtains in the art deco style of the 1920s and 1930s. Choose fabric with a horizontal zigzag or scalloped motif (as used here) to give the pelmet a decorative bottom edge. For an asymmetric effect, the curtains are tied back on one side only.

You will need

Basic Tool Kit (see page 13)

Standard long curtain pattern (see page 60), tie-back template and pelmet template (see page 62)

Fine cotton fabric with a suitable art deco pattern

Stiff card (cardstock)

Lightweight iron-on fabric interlining

Contrasting braid trim

Gold-coloured bead

Tip

Fabric that has been stiffened with iron-on interlining will not fray so there is no need to fray-check the bottom edge of the pelmet.

1 Make the curtains using the standard long curtain pattern and the instructions on pages 14–17. Pin the curtains to the pinning board and shape into folds with a knitting needle, draping one into a festoon for a tie-back. Steam and stiffen, then apply a card strip 20mm (³/₄in) deep to the back of the straight curtain.

2 Stiffen a small piece of fabric with iron-on interlining and cut out a tie-back using the template, positioning the pattern attractively. Glue on the braid trim, stitch in place around the draped curtain and attach a gold bead (see page 21). Cut a strip of stiff card 25mm (1in) wider than the window and glue the gathered tops of the curtains to this.

3 Using the template provided, cut out the pelmet in stiff card and score along the fold lines. Cut out a piece of fabric about 10mm (³/₈in) larger all round than the pelmet, ensuring that the lower scalloped or patterned edge will hang below the bottom edge of the pelmet and will be positioned symmetrically. Iron the interlining on to the back of the fabric to stiffen it.

4 Cut out along the patterned bottom edge and glue the fabric to the assembled pelmet (see page 38), with the bottom edge hanging down. Glue the curtains to the wall above the window so that they just touch the floor. Glue the pelmet over the top of the curtains.

Valance Curtains

Adding a valance to curtains gives a particularly rich look to a window, and the style is most suited to Victorian and modern dolls' houses. This project uses the same patterned fabric for the valance and curtains but looks equally attractive made with plain fabric and trimmed with embroidered ribbon or lace along the bottom of the valance.

You will need

Basic Tool Kit (see page 13)

Standard long curtain pattern, valance pattern (see page 60) and tie-back template (see page 62)

Fine cotton fabric with a suitable pattern

Matching soutache braid trim

Strip of thick cardboard or wood, 15mm (^{5}/$_8$in) wide and 25mm (1in) longer than the width of the window

1 Make the curtains using the standard long curtain pattern and the instructions on pages 14–17. Pull up the gathers to leave a gap between the curtains for a real window or without a gap for a faux window. Drape, steam and stiffen, then apply a card strip 20mm (^{3}/$_4$in) deep to the back of each curtain to hold the folds in place.

2 Cut out the valance using the template provided. Press down the top edge of the valance by 13mm (^{1}/$_2$in). Sew a line of gathering stitches 6mm (^{1}/$_4$in) from the folded edge and another 1.5mm (^{1}/$_{16}$in) below the first line of stitches.

3 Pull a longitudinal thread on the soutache braid to gather it into a frill, spreading the gathers evenly. Glue this to the bottom raw edge of the valance. Pull up the gathering threads on the valance until it is 13mm (^{1}/$_2$in) longer than the thick cardboard strip. Drape into gathers on the pinning board as for a curtain, steam and stiffen.

Tip

A valance is easy to drape in the same way as a full-length curtain – it is just a lot wider and shorter. Make sure that you keep the top gathered edge horizontal while you drape and pin the short vertical folds.

4 Glue the curtains to the cardboard or wood strip and glue the valance over the top, turning the raw ends under to fit and gluing them around the edges of the card. Glue the strip to the wall above the window.

Swag and Tails

This must be one of the most luxurious of window dressings and is not difficult to create in miniature. Swags and tails first appeared in the 18th century and have remained popular for formal rooms ever since. The sheer curtain in the project can be replaced with a plain blind, while matching drapes would be suitable for Victorian windows.

You will need

Basic Tool Kit (see page 13)

Large swag pattern, pelmet template and tail pattern (see pages 62–63)

Fine patterned fabric

Miniature fringe to match the lining

Contrasting silk fabric for lining

Stiff card (cardstock) for the pelmet

Fusible webbing

Voile full-length single curtain (see page 36)

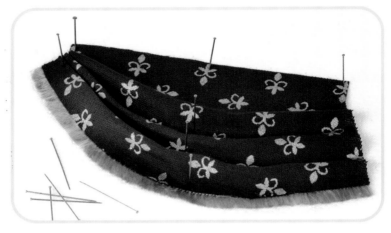

1 To make the swag, cut out the swag using the pattern provided, keeping the pattern symmetrical. Glue the fringe to the back of the curved lower edge. Pinch the fold lines into peaks down each side. Pin the top edge to the pinning board and pin down the pleated sides. Arrange the folds into flowing curves, pinning between each one. Steam and stiffen. When dry, remove from the board.

2 Trace the pelmet template on to stiff card and score along the fold lines. Cut out and assemble the pelmet, taping it together. Cover with patterned fabric (see page 38). Glue the top edge of the swag to the top of the pelmet.

Tip

This dressed window can be glued to any dolls' house room wall for a faux window effect. If the wall shows through the sheer voile, glue a rectangle of white card, the same size as the voile curtain, to the wall behind it.

3 To make the tails, cut out the tails using the pattern provided, making the second reversed, and positioning any pattern carefully so that the two halves match. Cut out a 15cm (6in) long by 25mm (1in) wide strip of lining. Lay a strip of fusible webbing along the angled bottom edge of each tail and lay the lining over it. Iron to bond the lining to the tail and trim the lining to match the tail. Glue fringe along the back of the diagonal edge of each tail.

4 Press back the side seams on each tail. Fold each tail along the fold lines and press firmly, holding each fold in place with a dab of PVA glue.

5 Glue the tails over the swag, gluing the top edge of each to the top of the pelmet with the sides of the tail curving around the sides of the pelmet. Fold the excess fabric at the top neatly under and glue down.

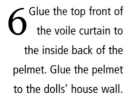

6 Glue the top front of the voile curtain to the inside back of the pelmet. Glue the pelmet to the dolls' house wall.

Grand Designs

The illustration shows how you can make a completely different look by reversing the patterned fabric and plain lining. Full-length curtains in the same yellow silk as the swag and tails make a sumptuous display that would be suitable for a Victorian or modern room. The swag is arranged over the tails in this design and is finished off with two polymer clay roundels.

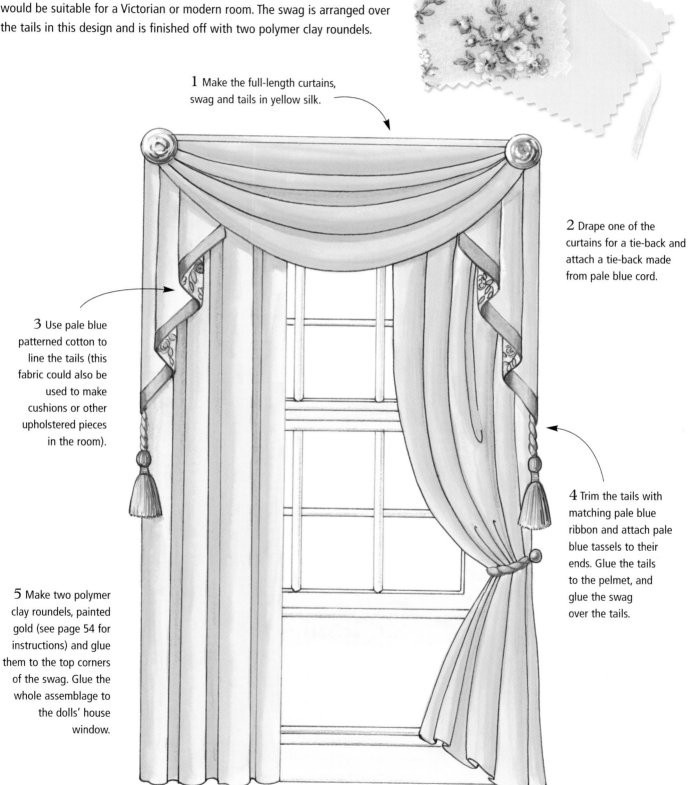

1 Make the full-length curtains, swag and tails in yellow silk.

2 Drape one of the curtains for a tie-back and attach a tie-back made from pale blue cord.

3 Use pale blue patterned cotton to line the tails (this fabric could also be used to make cushions or other upholstered pieces in the room).

4 Trim the tails with matching pale blue ribbon and attach pale blue tassels to their ends. Glue the tails to the pelmet, and glue the swag over the tails.

5 Make two polymer clay roundels, painted gold (see page 54 for instructions) and glue them to the top corners of the swag. Glue the whole assemblage to the dolls' house window.

Lambrequin

The lambrequin first appeared in the 18th century as a draped covering for the window surround and later developed into a hard pelmet with long sides. It is ideal for period drawing rooms or dining rooms and gives an elegant and formal effect. This project combines a lambrequin with sheer curtains, but you could use a simple full-length blind instead for a faux window.

You will need

Basic Tool Kit (see page 13)

Lambrequin template (see page 62) and standard long curtain pattern (see page 60)

Stiff card (cardstock)

Plain silk fabric in moss green

13mm (¹/₂in) wide ribbon with a woven pattern to match fabric:
- 2 lengths 15cm (6in) long
- 1 length 7.5cm (3in) long
- 2 lengths 5cm (2in) long

4 tassels in matching embroidery floss (see page 22)

Fine white silk for sheer curtains

Card strip, 10mm (³/₈in) wide and 11cm (4³/₈in) long

Variation

For a completely different look, cover the lambrequin with patterned fabric and glue matching braid around the edges.

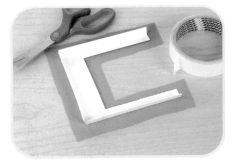

1 Using the template provided, cut out the lambrequin in stiff card and score along the fold lines. Fold to shape and tape with masking tape. Cut a piece of green silk large enough to cover the lambrequin and apply with PVA glue as for the pelmet on page 38.

2 Brush diluted glue on 13mm (¹/₂in) of one end of each of the two long and two short lengths of ribbon to prevent fraying. When dry, cut the end into a point. Stitch a tassel to each point.

3 Glue the 7.5cm (3in) length of ribbon vertically to the centre front of the lambrequin, tucking the ends under and gluing firmly. Glue the long lengths to the front sides of the lambrequin so that the point with the tassel hangs below the lower edge. Glue the remaining two tasselled ribbons on either side of the centre ribbon in the same way.

4 Make up two full-length sheer curtains using the standard long curtain pattern (see page 60) and the instructions on pages 14–18. Gather them up to leave a gap between them as though partly drawn. Glue the tops to the card strip and glue the strip to the wall above the window. Glue the lambrequin over the top of the curtains.

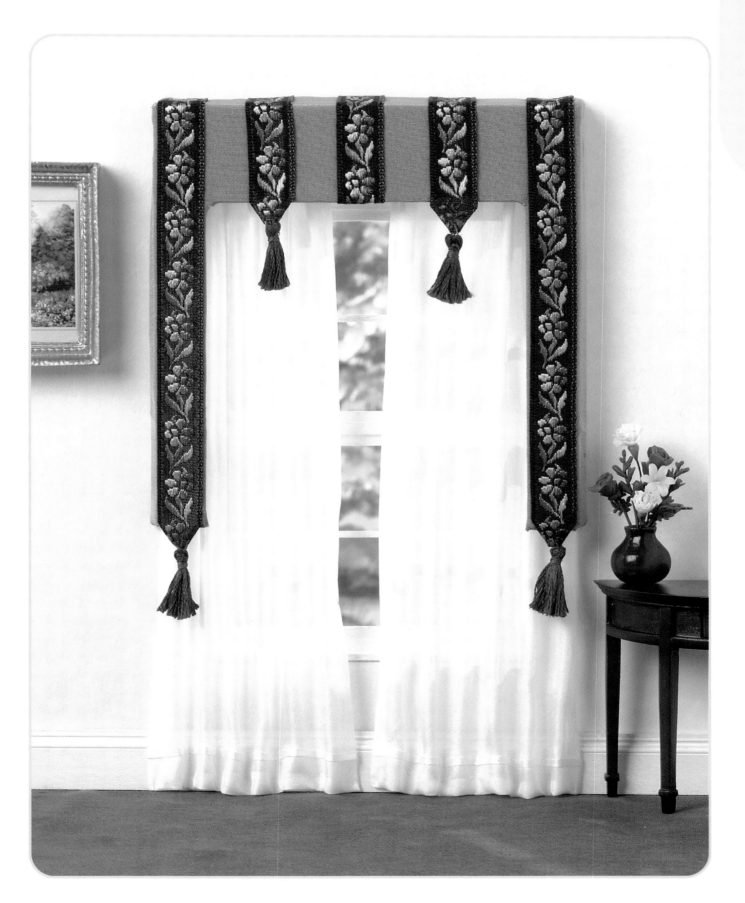

Café Curtain

Probably invented in Vienna in the 19th century, café curtains have been popular ever since, and this pretty tab-topped curtain would be ideal for a miniature teashop or café. It looks best made in a striped or patterned fabric because it lacks fullness, and you can embellish it further with added trims and bows. The curtain should be about half the height of the window.

You will need

Basic Tool Kit (see page 13)

Pattern (see page 63)

Graph paper

Fine striped cotton fabric

Wooden skewer or dowelling, 3mm (1/8in) diameter, painted brown

Patterned ribbon trim to match fabric

3mm (1/8in) braid to match fabric

Two round knob finials in mid brown (see page 20)

Hooks (optional)

Tip

Café curtains are also a popular alternative to net curtains for bedrooms and look very pretty in a floral print. You could make them using added tabs of ribbon instead of cut out tabs. See the Hanging Tapestry project on page 26 for instructions on how to glue tabs to the back.

1 Trace the café curtain pattern on to graph paper to ensure that the loops are accurate. Measure the width of the window and adjust the pattern so that it is 13mm (1/2in) wider than the window and 20mm (3/4in) longer than half the height. Cut out the curtain but do not cut out the scalloped top yet. Glue up a hem of 10mm (3/8in) along the bottom edge.

2 Using dilute PVA glue, paint the top 25mm (1in) of the curtain and a line along the side edges. When the glue is completely dry, lay the template on the curtain and draw round the tabbed top edge with a sharp pencil. Use sharp scissors to cut out the tabs as accurately as possible; the dried glue will prevent fraying.

3 Lay the curtain face down and lay the skewer along the centre of the row of protruding tabs. Apply dabs of glue to the base of each tab and press the tab down over the skewer on to the glue to secure.

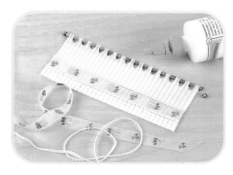

4 Glue the ribbon trim to the right side of the curtain and a line of braid above and below the ribbon to accent it. Trim the skewer to just longer than the width of the curtain and glue on the finials. Finally, glue the pole to the wall on either side of the window, or use hooks (see page 32).

Curtains for a Bay Window

Dolls' houses often have bay windows, usually at the front of the house, and these require curtains that look good both from the outside and the inside. This project is an easy way to curtain a bay window by fixing curtains with tie-backs at either side and using a valance to give the illusion that the curtains can be drawn round the bay.

You will need

Basic Tool Kit (see page 13)

Curtain pattern (see page 61) and valance (see page 62)

Fine cotton fabric in a small print

Fine white lace: 10mm (³/₈in) wide and 35.5cm (14in) long

Thin card (cardstock)

2 gold-coloured beads

1 Cut out the curtains using the pattern and glue the side and bottom hems. Sew two lines of gathering threads 3mm (¹/₈in) from the top edge of each curtain and pull up the gathers until it is the width of a side window. Pin and drape for tie-backs, then steam and stiffen.

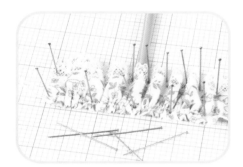

2 Cut out and make up the valance using the pattern provided. Glue a line of fine lace along the bottom and sew the first line of gathering thread 1.5mm (¹/₁₆in) from the hemmed top edge. Pull up the gathers so that the valance will fit all round the inside of the bay plus 6mm (¹/₄in). Pin, drape, steam and stiffen. Glue each side under 3mm (¹/₈in) to neaten.

3 Cut two card strips, the width of the top of each curtain and 13mm (¹/₂in) deep. Glue the top of each curtain to one of these. Make tie-backs from the lace and stitch to the curtains with a gold-coloured bead.

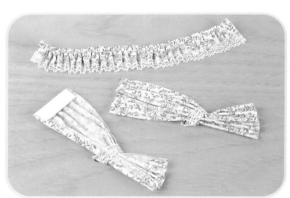

Measurements

The patterns given are for a dolls' house bay window with an inside opening of 11cm (4³/₈in) wide and 12cm (4³/₄in) high. If your bay window is a different size, adjust the curtain and valance patterns accordingly (see Measuring miniature windows, page 14).

4 Glue the card-backed tops of the curtains in place above the side windows of the bay, bending the card slightly to fit if necessary around any curves. Glue the valance over the tops of the curtains all round the inside of the bay. Glue the beaded end of each tie-back to the edge of each window.

Elaborate Curtains

These sumptuous curtains, popular in the Regency and Victorian periods as well as today, would suit the grandest dolls' house and are topped with a golden cornice. The cornice is decorated with polymer clay roundels for a truly opulent effect. This elaborate curtain is intended as a faux window display to be glued to the back wall of a dolls' house room.

You will need

Basic Tool Kit (see page 13)

Small swag pattern (see page 63), standard long curtain pattern (see page 60), tie-back template, cornice mounting template (see page 62)

1:12 scale dolls' house cornice, 10mm (³⁄₈in) wide (see Tip)

Razor saw or hacksaw

Sandpaper

Beige polymer clay

Charms or small pieces of jewellery

Large needle

Gold acrylic paint

Gold slub silk fabric

Black double picot braid trim

2 gold-coloured beads

Black-and-gold brocade or jacquard fabric

Stiff card (cardstock) for the cornice mounting

2 black tassels on 5cm (2in) long cords (see page 22)

Tip

Miniature dolls' house wooden mouldings, such as the cornice used here, are available from dolls' house suppliers. Cornice is usually sold in 30cm (12in) lengths. You will need enough to make a 13cm (5in) long cornice for this project.

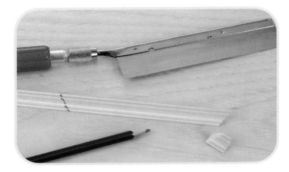

1 Measure a 13cm (5in) length of cornice and mark the cutting lines on the top of the cornice at 45-degree angles. Cut the ends along these lines. (You can use a mitre block if you have one, but this is not essential.) Sand the ends smooth.

2 Form two 6mm (¹⁄₄in) balls of polymer clay into ovals and press them vertically on to each end of the front of the cornice. Press a charm into the centre of each and remove it to make an impressed image. Form a 10mm (³⁄₈in) ball of clay into an oval and press horizontally on to the centre of the cornice. Impress as before and decorate around the edge with the eye of a large needle.

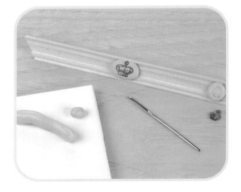

3 Bake the roundels on the cornice for about 15 minutes at 130°C/275°F/Gas ½, or according to the manufacturers' instructions on the polymer clay packet. When cool, glue the roundels firmly in place, if necessary, and paint the whole cornice gold.

4 Cut out the swag and fray-check the edges. Glue a line of black picot braid to the curved bottom edge. Make the swag according to the instructions on page 44. Make the curtains using the standard long curtain pattern and the instructions on pages 15–19, pinning and draping them for tie-backs.

5 Make the curved tie-backs from the gold silk following the instructions on page 21 and trim them with picot braid. Stitch each to a curtain with a bead to hold it.

6 Cut out the blind from the brocade or jacquard fabric to measure 20 x 11cm (8 x 4³/₈in) or to fit the window, and paint the sides and top edges with dilute PVA glue. Use a pin to pull out threads from the bottom edge to fray it to a depth of about 13mm (¹/₂in).

7 Use the cornice mounting template provided to cut out the cornice mount in card and score along the fold lines. Paint the outside of the mount with gold paint. Glue the top edge of the blind to the inside back of the mount, and then glue the tops of the curtains over it. Glue the tassels to the outer tops of the curtains.

8 Glue the swag over the curtains and the tassels. Fold in the side and top flaps of the mount and glue in place. Glue the cornice to the front of the mount and glue the whole assembly to the wall of the dolls' house room.

Soft and Exotic

This alternative to the Elaborate Curtains would be suitable for a Regency or Victorian dolls' house and has a valance instead of a swag below a white and gold cornice.

1 Cut a piece of cornice to length and glue a piece of 10mm (³⁄₈in) wide lace to the front. Paint the cornice and lace with white acrylic paint and, when dry, pick out the detail of the lace in gold paint to suggest an elaborate moulding.

2 Cut out and make a single full-length curtain, half as wide again as the window. Trim the right side and bottom with gold fringe and gather it up to fit the width of the window.

3 Drape to the left for a tie-back and attach a matching tie-back.

4 Make a valance using the pattern from the Valance Curtains project on page 42 and trim with gold fringe.

5 Assemble the curtains and cornice with two gold tassels hanging down on the right side. Glue the whole assembly to the dolls' house window.

Curtains Aren't Just for Windows

The projects in this book can be adapted to make curtains for all kinds of furnishings. Here are some examples from different rooms of the dolls' house.

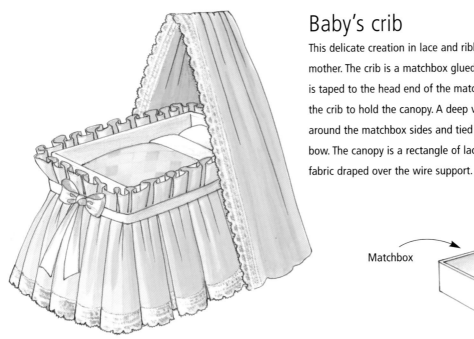

Baby's crib

This delicate creation in lace and ribbon would delight any dolls' house mother. The crib is a matchbox glued to a cotton reel. A length of stiff wire is taped to the head end of the matchbox and bent at a right angle over the crib to hold the canopy. A deep valance is glued around the matchbox sides and tied with a ribbon bow. The canopy is a rectangle of lace-trimmed fabric draped over the wire support.

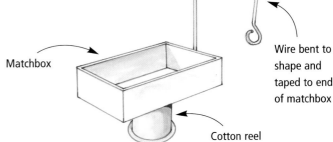

Matchbox

Wire bent to shape and taped to end of matchbox

Cotton reel

Dressing table and matching stool

A softly feminine dressing table is made using a 6mm (¼in) thick balsa sheet cut out in the shape of a kidney top and glued to the top of a large cotton reel. The curtain is made and glued around the table top with embroidered ribbon glued over the raw edges to finish it off. The stool is a cotton reel with a padded piece of contrasting fabric glued to the top and a curtain fixed around the outside, as for the dressing table. A purchased mirror completes the set.

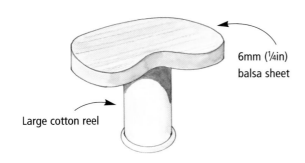

6mm (¼in) balsa sheet

Large cotton reel

Canopied bed

Beds with canopies of the kind shown here have been used for grand bedrooms since medieval times. This miniature version is made using a single gathered curtain, lined in a contrasting fabric. Make a ring of stiff card (cardstock) and glue the gathered top of the curtain around the inside. Glue the ring to the wall with the opening side of the curtains to the front. Press a drawing pin into the wall on either side of the bed to hold the curtains open.

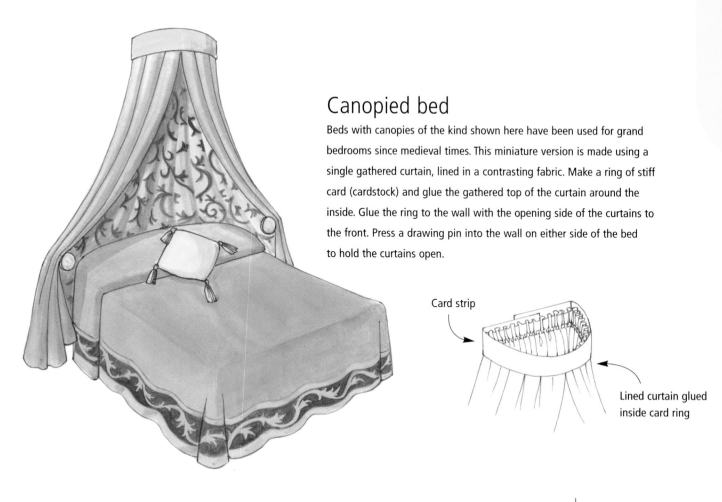

Card strip

Lined curtain glued inside card ring

Shower curtain

A shower curtain adds softness to a miniature bathroom and is not difficult to make. Use thin plastic or nylon fabric and glue tabs to the top as for Hanging Tapestry on page 26. Thread the tabs on to a length of wire and bend it to shape to make a shower rail. Drill small holes into the wall and glue the ends of the wire into these.

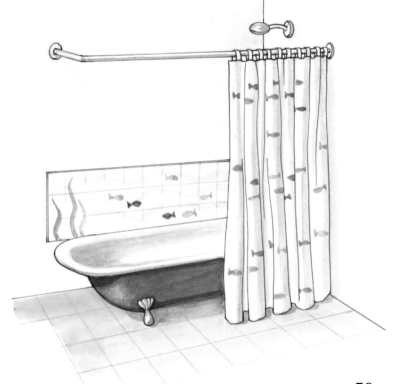

Templates and Patterns

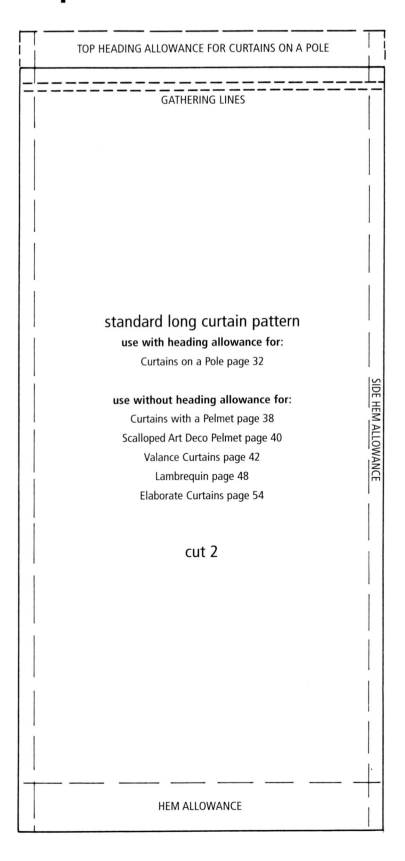

TOP HEADING ALLOWANCE FOR CURTAINS ON A POLE

GATHERING LINES

standard long curtain pattern

use with heading allowance for:

Curtains on a Pole page 32

use without heading allowance for:

Curtains with a Pelmet page 38

Scalloped Art Deco Pelmet page 40

Valance Curtains page 42

Lambrequin page 48

Elaborate Curtains page 54

cut 2

SIDE HEM ALLOWANCE

HEM ALLOWANCE

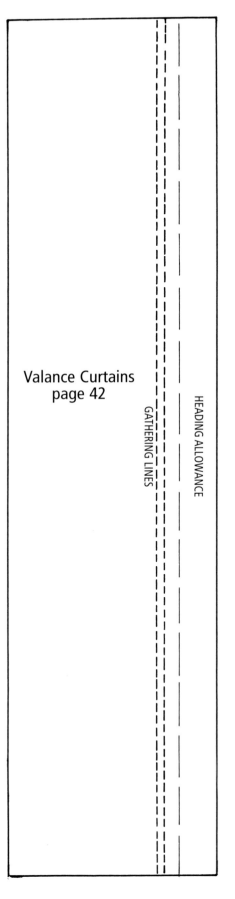

Valance Curtains
page 42

GATHERING LINES

HEADING ALLOWANCE

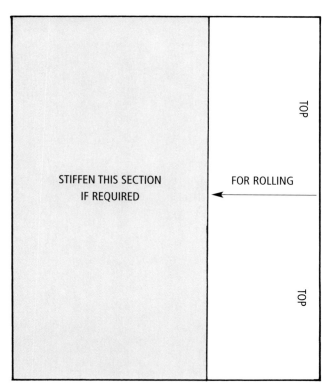

TOP

STIFFEN THIS SECTION
IF REQUIRED

FOR ROLLING

TOP

Roller Blind page 28

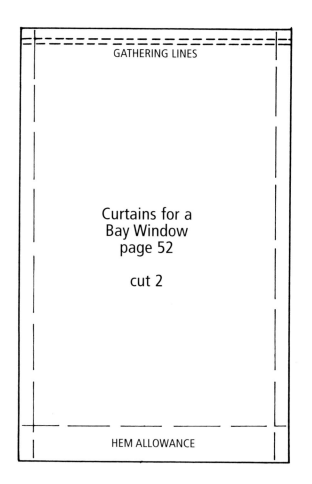

GATHERING LINES

Curtains for a
Bay Window
page 52

cut 2

HEM ALLOWANCE

Hanging Tapestry page 26

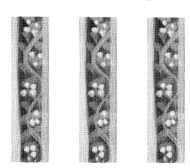

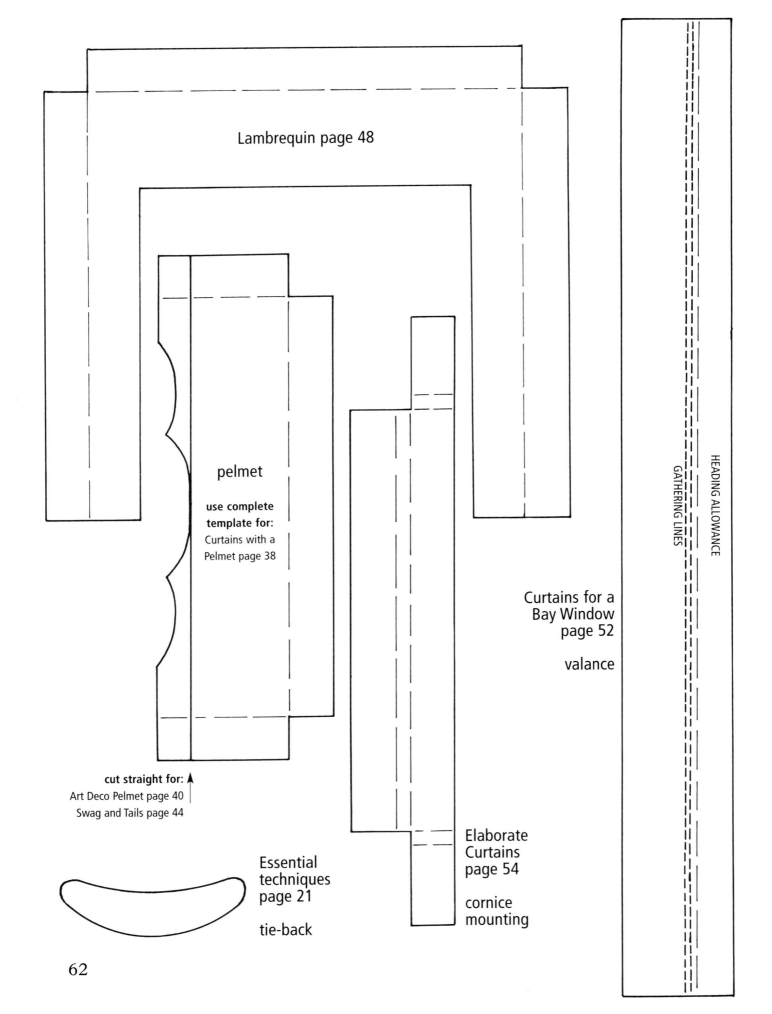

Lambrequin page 48

pelmet

**use complete
template for:**
Curtains with a
Pelmet page 38

cut straight for: ↑
Art Deco Pelmet page 40
Swag and Tails page 44

Essential
techniques
page 21

tie-back

Curtains for a
Bay Window
page 52

valance

Elaborate
Curtains
page 54

cornice
mounting

GATHERING LINES

HEADING ALLOWANCE

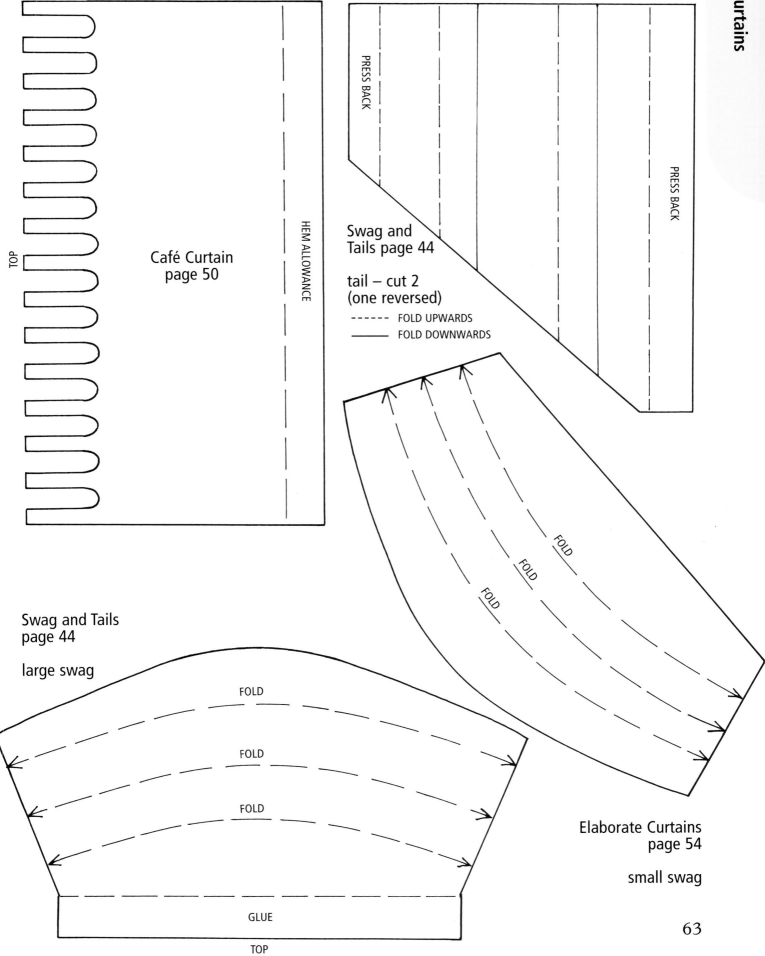

TOP

Café Curtain
page 50

HEM ALLOWANCE

PRESS BACK

PRESS BACK

Swag and
Tails page 44

tail – cut 2
(one reversed)

- - - - - - FOLD UPWARDS
———— FOLD DOWNWARDS

FOLD

FOLD

FOLD

Swag and Tails
page 44

large swag

FOLD

FOLD

FOLD

Elaborate Curtains
page 54

small swag

GLUE

TOP

63

Suppliers

Fabric and trimmings are widely available from fabric and haberdashery sections of major department stores as well as craft and hobby suppliers. For fabrics and trimmings chosen specially for the miniaturist, the following suppliers are highly recommended and provide a mail-order service worldwide:

UK
Dixie Collection
PO Box 575
Bromley
Kent
BR2 7WP
tel/fax: 020 8462 0700
www.dixiecollection.co.uk

USA
Sandy's Lace and Trims
7417 N. Knoxville Ave.
Peoria
IL 61614
tel: (309) 689-1943
fax: (309) 689-1942
www.sandyslace.com

Photo: Tamsin Heaser

About the author

Sue Heaser has worked professionally in crafts for over 20 years. After a globetrotting childhood, Sue studied at art college and university in England. She then worked as an archaeological illustrator before turning to a career as a highly versatile craft writer, designer and teacher. Her skills range from polymer clay miniatures, dolls and jewellery to candlemaking, puppetry, ceramics and textiles. This is Sue's eleventh craft book, and she is the author of *Dolls House DIY: Food Displays*, also published by David & Charles.

Acknowledgments

We would like to thank Dolls House Emporium for the use of their accessories: washbasin page 29; table page 35; chair page 43; table and picture page 49; chairs page 51; lamp and picture page 55. For your free catalogue of the complete range contact The Dolls House Emporium, quoting EDC4 at:

The Dolls House Emporium
EDC4, Ripley
Derbyshire, DE5 3YD
tel: 01773 514400
www.dollshouse.com

All other accessories were made or provided by the author.

Index